The Learning
of
LOVE

Simon Parke has worked for Sainsbury's and Spitting Image
and is now working for the Church of England. He has also
Paused for Thought with Terry Wogan, run the
London Marathon and written three novels:
Desert Depths, Desert Ascent *and* Desert Child;
and One-Minute Mystic, *a forerunner of this book.*
He is married with two children and
lives in North London.

One Heart. We are.

The Learning *of* LOVE

Simon Parke

First published in Great Britain in 2000
Azure
1 Marylebone Road
London NW1 4DU

British Library Cataloguing-in-Publication Data

A catalogue record for this book is available from the British Library

ISBN 1-902694-06-6

Typeset in Benguiat by
Pioneer Associates, Perthshire
Printed in Malta by
Interprint Limited

 **THE EASY LIFE**

If you want an easy life, choose something simple
and relatively undemanding.
Go and swim the English Channel,
there and back, mid-January.
Navigate a yacht around the world, blindfold,
or a log raft down the Amazon,
with no crocodile repellent on board.
Run a marathon, weekly, or raise the *Titanic*, solo.
Take up regular SAS survival courses on the Brecon
Beacons, insisting the easy bits be taken out.
Climb K2 and Everest with just an
extra woolly jumper for the cold.
Traverse the Arctic Circle in slippers,
jog the Sahara with weights.

As I say, if you want an easy life,
choose something simple and relatively undemanding.
But if you fancy a challenge,
choose the Learning of Love.

SOCIALLY ACCEPTABLE

Some people think the opposite
of love is hate.
You, of course, are wiser than that.
You know that the opposite
of love is indifference.

Indifference kills,
because it contains no energy for reaching out.
But it's a socially acceptable drug,
so most of us get away with it.

Social murder.
But no police on our case . . .

 # CONFESSIONS

After a long period in my life during which
I felt nothing which was hopeful,
nothing which was intimate,
nothing which was healing,
I finally gave myself permission to
ask God the question:

What's in this for me?

It's generally considered a selfish question.
For me, it was Life.

As the proverb says,
Hope deferred makes the heart sick,
but a desire fulfilled is a tree of life.

The wick needs the wax. The fish needs the chips.
And I needed to experience hope,
intimacy, healing, *something!* –
if I was to love again.

SHOWER ME THE WAY

Fa-la-la, tra-la-la, fa-la-la-laa,
dee-dum-dee-do
tum-ti-tum-tum-tum-ti-tum
did-diddly-do, did-diddly-do . . .

Sometimes when we're in the shower,
the actual words don't matter too much, frankly.
We just want to sing.
We can remember the first line,
and maybe the second, but after that?
Who knows?!
So tum-ti-tum-ti-tum.
And very good it sounds too.

And life reflects the shower.
We needn't be afraid of situations
in which we don't feel we have the right words.
We just need the right heart.
Everything else is secondary.

In the words of The Great Sage,
Da-doo-ron-ron-ron, da-doo-ron-ron.

THE CHEMISTRY SET

I wanted to buy you this chemistry set, Melvin.
Thank you Auntie, but –
I looked at it and I thought, 'That's for Melvin!'
Well, it's kind, but –
I was fascinated by it – took me back to my
own childhood, you see!
That's nice, Auntie.
I used to love my chemistry set. All the
little bits and bobs, the different colours of the
chemicals, the distinctive smells!
Really.
Oh yes. It was given to me by my Uncle Jim.
Always my favourite uncle of course. Always
gave me the *best* presents! –
But I don't like chemistry.
– And you'll also like this. It's a book about
the *history* of chemistry. I stood in the shop
for hours reading it!

Love is the accurate assessment of others' need.
Not your own.
Your great acts of love.
Who are they for exactly?

 WASTE

After he walked out,
she lit a candle.
It burnt in the window on the stairs.
A light of welcome.
A light of welcome home.
A light of please come back.

It burnt for years.
He never saw it.
Never knew of it.
And then she died.

Such a waste of wax.
Such a waste of time.

But then love is wasteful.
They say the most beautiful flower ever created
lived and died in a forest
and was seen by

no one.

THE ENERGY

The experience of love is energy.
Energy to face the hopeless Mondays
the energy to walk in the rain
to laugh in dull meetings
to miss lunch
to be strong for others
to find the positive
to take the crap
to offer welcome
to grasp the nettle
to contemplate the impossible
to laugh at fear
to be open to failure
to say 'yes' to the future.

The experience of love is energy.
The energy to look death in the eye
and call it 'friend'.

But where there is no experience of love . . .

THE HARDEST BIT OF ALL

The first bit wasn't so hard.
I loved my child.
Cared. Nurtured. Possessed.

But the second bit?
The letting go of my child? The gradual separation?
It's like organizing my own death:
signing my own death warrant.

I thought love was about two becoming one.
But this is about one becoming two.
And it's ripping me apart.
Literally.

Within the loving mother,
there needs to be a loving woman.
And the woman will need to help the mother.
Because this second bit
is the hardest bit of all.

 A GENTLE PLACE

In the learning of love,
you'll need a gentle place,
to which you can go,
when the wounds seem too much to bear.

A place where the speaking is honest,
the confusion is acknowledged,
and the hurt is bathed.

It could be a person.
It could be a prayer.
But when you know your life hugged
you know you are there.

THE OBVIOUS

Let's state the obvious.
Love only works if two people
communicate from the centre of their being.
Each in touch with their own centre.
And each prepared to accept whatever lies
at the heart of their partner.

For only here is reality, life, depth.
Here is conflict also.
But conflict which grows into something.
As opposed to conflict which just avoids the real issues.

Staying with the obvious,
when one or both are *unable* to live from their centres,
then it isn't love. It's an *arrangement*.
An arrangement for co-existence.
A making-do.
It might survive.
Might bring moderate happiness.

But let's not call it *love*.
Wouldn't want to cheapen the word, would we?

COMPROMISING SITUATIONS

Suppose you love the foreign spy –
and you love your country he is undermining?

Suppose you love both your parents,
but they hate each other?

Suppose you love different people
in different ways for different reasons?

Suppose you love the man who hits you.
Or the woman who walked out on you.

Suppose you love those you are not meant to love?
The love that dares not speak its name.

Love.
It's compromising.

 **DEAF WISH**

Most listening doesn't involve our ears.

You can listen for logic, for reason, with your mind.
You can listen for emotional truth with your heart.
You can listen for energy with your gut.
You can listen out for the past through smell and scent.
You can listen for fear by looking in the child's eyes.
You can listen for body-truth through touch.
You can listen for your neighbour, by putting
yourself in their shoes.

There are many ways of being deaf.
And most of them don't involve ears.

 **GUSTAVE**

In 1869, the French writer Gustave Flaubert
wrote to Princess Mathilde that it was proving to
be a good year for him. It was in fact the beginning
of the end.

Five weeks later, his friend Louis Bouilet died;
shortly after, the critics turned on his latest work;
1870 brought the death of another friend, Jules Duplan,
and then in 1872, he lost his mother. When the timber prices
collapsed, ruining him financially, his health,
never good, finally cracked. By 1875, Gustave
was a broken man.

However gifted or determined we are,
life is infinitely fragile. Love lives now.
Tomorrow may be very different.

COMING TOGETHER

Love isn't the result of sexual happiness.
Sexual happiness *might* be the result of love.

The frigid woman.
The impotent man.
Crucified by the inhibitions within,
which make it impossible to love.
They fear the other sex.
Or hate the other sex.
So in that moment of spontaneity,
of physical connection,
the brakes slam,
the wheels lock,
they cannot give, they cannot trust.
No coming together here . . .

Love isn't the result of sexual happiness.
But sexual happiness *might* be the result of love.

IN CASE OF FIRE

If you don't want anyone to read
what you've written, put
'In case of fire' at the top of the page,
and stick it in a very public place.
No one will read about what isn't going to happen,
and which just states the very obvious anyway.

Oh. And here's another thing.
If you don't want anyone to listen to you,
just use the word 'love' a lot,
so that it means everything and nothing,
and most things in between.

All you need is love!

Absolutely.

 # FOR THE KIDS

We're staying together for the kids.
Don't want to deprive them of a stable home.
It's something *we* both appreciated
when we were growing up.

So, the unhappiness will continue.
The awful tension in the air.
The petty sniping, the strained atmosphere.
The small conflicts which just disguise
the real conflict.
The terrible silences.
The shallow, awkward communication.
The pervading sense that everyone is walking on eggshells.
The occasional violence.

It's for the kids.
And one day they'll be grateful.

Of course.
Just as I wake up grateful for my nightmares.
So grateful.

 BARRY

He had a room-temperature IQ.
Bright as Alaska in December.
If brains were taxed, he'd get a rebate.
A large one.
Must have got into the gene pool while
the lifeguard wasn't watching.
He had the wisdom of youth,
and the energy of old age.
The evolutionary process had clearly
built a bypass around his house.
He'd reached rock-bottom a long time ago –
and continued to dig.

The gates were down, the lights flashing –
but there was no train coming.
You know what they said of Barry:
that he was depriving a village somewhere of an idiot.

This was all true, of course.
But I loved Barry.
Because he was the only one who made me tea
when I made deliveries to his office . . .

DOING THE HONOURABLE THING

Bit nervous.
They're opening the present now.
I hope they like it.
I tried so hard in the shop to imagine
what they might want.
Not what *I* might want.
What *they* might want.

It's not easy buying a CD when
you feel there's only one half-decent track on it.
Not easy at all. Not at that price.
Goes against the grain.
But that's love, I suppose.

'So, er, do you like it?'
'Honestly?'
'Honestly.'
'No. I think it's crap.'

Failure.
But at least it's *honourable* failure.
I tried.

HOME, SWEET HOME

I love the way you don't put
the top back on the toothpaste.
I love the way you act as though
it's only you who's done any work today.
I love the way you always start with a
criticism.
I love the way you contradict me in
front of the children.
I love you when you're ill, and behave as
though the entire resources of the
NHS are but a drop in the ocean compared
to your great need.
I love it when you sit in a mood
in the kitchen.
I love the way you imagine your dirty
socks will make their own way to the washing machine.
I love it when you snore.

Meanwhile, back on planet earth . . .

THE FIRST OFFENCE

As the murderer is sentenced,
as he stands in the dock,
as he remembers his offence –
he half-remembers another,
committed many moons before . . .

His dad would say,
'Tough love.'
His mum would say,
'It never did me any harm.'
And there followed the first offence, m'lud.
Little feelings murdered.
Little child silenced.
Buried in the past.
Never really searched for.
And never really found.

There in the dock, on this sunny morning,
two offences.
There in the dock, as the cameras wait,
Monster *and* victim.

Caught. Dismissed.

 IS THIS IT?

They looked everywhere.
They looked in the streets.
They looked in the hills.
They looked in the car parks, schools and shops.

They looked in their homes.
They looked in the desert, and in the sea.
They looked in the office.
They looked behind the sofa cushion where things usually
were.
At the bus stop.
In the playground.
Down the mines.
North, South, East and West, they looked.
On the moon. In the stars.
And behind the bushes near the bike sheds.

They looked everywhere.
No stone unturned.
But no luck. Exhausted, they gave up.
They hadn't found it.

Not that anyone knew what they were looking for, of course.
And that can make a search a lot harder.

 # HELL OF A DAY

When he died, and went to hell,
several local residents signed a petition for his release,
and took it to the appropriate authorities.
It made no difference.
They hurried home. It was very hot.

So his local MP went to lobby on his behalf.
Let him out! he demanded, rattling the gates.
But no one was really listening.
He hurried home. It was very hot.

So his dad went to visit.
Didn't say anything.
Just burnt his hands opening the gates,
scalded his face by stepping inside,
and sweated blood carrying him out.
And home.

Love.
It enters the hell of others.
As opposed to posturing on the sidelines.

 MY BEST FRIEND

Since you left, I've cried anger, sadness and despair.
Hot headache sobbing which heals nothing.

They say, 'You've always got the memories!'
Indeed.
Unfortunately, each one – it laughs in my face.
Because I can't hold its hand.
Or look into its eyes.
Or share its sandwich.

They say my tears will water a garden.
Maybe.
But at the moment the ground is very hard.

I hate self-pity.
But in my better moments, I can almost forgive myself.
Because since you left,
I know what I've lost. I know who I've lost.

My hero.
My best friend.

A COMMITTEE RELATIONSHIP

From what I remember of the story,
the man wanted to have sex with the woman.
But he couldn't.
Or rather, it would be difficult.
Because he was a priest, and meant to be celibate.
And she was a nun.

So instead, he put her on a committee.

Repressed desire.
It probably explains the composition
of a large number of committees,
all over the world.

FEELING IN THE *MOOD* . . .

After the game, the coach of the
opposing team said to Bill,
'You were lucky today.
You've been lucky all season.'
And Bill said,
'Yes, the more we practise, the luckier we seem to get!'

After the performance,
the gushing groupie said to the maestro,
'It must be lovely to be able
to play the piano like that!'
And the maestro said,
'Yes – it's about eight hours' practice a day lovely.'

If you're waiting till you're in the *mood* for love,
don't imagine you're taking the business very seriously.
Love is discipline.
Love is work.

HOSPITALITY SWEET

Thank you for joining me in my world.
Thank you for stooping so low to enter.
Thank you for standing here with me,
while I show you my little collection of pictures,
memories, mistakes, triumphs and sadnesses.

Thank you for not being too eager to get home.
Thank you for not telling me all about *your*
front room; thank you for not bringing
your collection of pictures and memories,
knowing they would crowd out mine.
Thank you for not feeling the need to give
me advice.

Thank you. You are a friend, who, for me,
looks and feels very much like God.

 OPPOSITES

He loved her.
He doted on her.
She was everything to him.
To the exclusion of everything and everyone else.
Such love!

Such drivel.
The parish priest was glad to escape.
The claustrophobic funeral visit
had been a monologue of expanded egotism. Not love.

Love is an attitude towards the world.
Not a closed shop around one other.

To be frank,
if my love for one
doesn't inspire me outwards into love for all,
it's an evil love.
It is the stench of the rotting lily.

DOWNWARDLY MOBILE

I was talking when she said it.
Your mobile, she said –
it's breaking up.

But I wasn't on the mobile.
It was just me.
Me breaking up.
Me breaking down,
in confusion and pain.

Love gives life.
It can also take it away.

LITTLE BOYS IN LONG TROUSERS

She was 34 when she finally left home.

She'd physically left years before.
But somehow she'd gone on being
intimidated, frightened –
and it was *her* who apologized
when her dad threw his tantrums, and stamped his little feet.

No more.

Grown men who are still
emotionally little boys,
are not best served by their daughters playing mum.

The loving thing is to leave the power of home,
walk free, declare enough is enough.
Draw a line.

*If he is to be blessed,
the little boy must face himself . . .*

 # IN THE BEGINNING

First of all, love greets.
In those early moments,
love welcomes.

In the beginning,
love establishes safety for the other.
Love establishes space for the other.

To give such love is to die a little, of course,
but to *receive* it?
Well – it's like stepping into a sunlit
playground after triple maths . . .

 UNREASONABLE

She'd rung, I'd picked up the phone,
and we were having a nice chat.
It was good to hear her.
I was telling her how I was.
She was telling me how she was.
But I suppose all along,
at the back of my mind,
I was waiting for her to get to the point.
Waiting for the reason.

And then the bombshell.
The big news.
I just thought I'd ring, she said.
No particular reason.

I was shell-shocked, of course.
Fighting for breath on the end of the phone.
That someone could ring me
for no particular reason.

When there doesn't have to be a reason,
maybe we're in the foothills of love.

A FRIEND IN NEED . . .

My uncle Tom was straight into action.
Phoning round. He was good like that.
Anything he could do for you.
No one else I know could have had
an electrician, a carpet salesman,
a locksmith, a glazier,
a car mechanic, a mountaineer,
an insurance rep., a horse breeder,
a bishop, two hairdressers,
a travel agent, a dog handler,
a ski instructor, a quiz show host
and a wine importer from Gwent,
on my doorstep within the hour.

Unfortunately none proved very helpful
in the unblocking of my drain.
What I actually needed was a plumber.

Love is the *accurate* assessment of need.

THE PLAYGROUND

When the children were told
that they couldn't play there,
they were very sad.
Because it was their favouritest
playground in all the whole world.
Utterly. Completely.
And their sadness was overwhelming.
For every day they passed it.
And every day, the gate said No.
And every day seemed only half a life,
amidst the hopeless longing.

You can't take the playground out of the child.
You can't take the longings from the human heart.

Living the pain of the unfulfilled,
without it destroying you or others;
living it kindly and gently –
well, the learning of love doesn't get much harder than this . . .

 A PAINFUL LIMP

Snake's blood is quite a good aphrodisiac, apparently,
and used in eastern Asia.
Obviously it needs to be fresh,
which may be a problem. Depends where you shop.

Or powdered rhino horn.
Strongly recommended by a Chinese emperor,
who entertained his court by balancing
women on his erect member.
(No one you know. This was 3000 years ago.)

Then there's Spanish Fly of course.
Made from the remains of
the emerald green blister beetle.
Yummy.
A legendary aphrodisiac certainly.
But also the cause of serious poisoning.

Do aphrodisiacs really work?
That's a hard one.
Or rather, sometimes it isn't.

Which is why the desperate search goes on . . .

NAME AND SHAME

So this bloke is banging nails through my wrists.
Bastard. 'Scuse my French,
but the pain is exploding in my brain,
my scream too loud for me to hear.
They'd planned this. Three years of hate.
Three years of jealousy, fear,
sniping from every angle,
poisoning everything positive.
Well, they've won. And I've lost.
Surprise, surprise.

My cross is being swung skywards,
and all that's left for me
is to name and shame, speak my mind.
Here goes, hear this!

*'Forgive them, Father – they don't
know what they are doing.'*

Jesus never could say the right thing.

 **NEVER**

Never say 'I love you.'
You might be asked to prove it.

The cuddly toy on Valentine's day,
the romantic comedy at the Odeon,
and the Mexican on the corner,
where you laugh and dance the night away,
fuelled by rum, Coke and lust –
the temptation's so strong, but don't.
Don't say it.

Never say 'I love you.'
You might be asked to prove it.
You might be asked to die for them.
And laying down your life for someone
can really ruin a good night out . . .

 THE LEPER

I take a photo from the box.
Bad choice. It's that little boy.
No front teeth, and picking his nose.
That stupid know-it-all smirk,
and the ill-fitting clothes
he thought so cool.

It is me. Long ago. Once upon a time.
I've grown up now of course.
Moved on.
Well thank God for that!
But how embarrassing all the same.
A little figure, enthroned
at the centre of his own pathetic little universe.
And really quite ugly.

I put the leper back in the box.
Quickly now.
I bury the leper beneath a hundred other prints.
Move on, move on.

But until I can befriend that leper,
I can befriend no one.

 # THE ROOM

It's a warm room.
Inside the colours glow.
There's a log fire,
flickering silent images dance across the wall,
and the sofa,
the candles,
and the hand is held,
and the life is shared,
and the passion burns,
and the two are two,
yet the two are also one.

The smiles, the laughter,
the honesty fearless and easy,
and the sex that eases the ache.

But I am locked out of that room.
I have beaten my fists against the door, till sore.
It's cold out here . . .

THE GOOD CRISIS

Love proceeds by no assured plan.
Everything is crisis,
everything is a moment of decision,
for parents, partners, friends.
Everything is risk, adjustment, precarious.
Will the result be tragedy – or triumph? No one knows.

For there are no blueprints on offer,
no generalizations to be made.
There is no one on hand to say,
'In this situation, this rule applies.'
There is no chart on the wall,
marking progress.

There is just the real life situation you inhabit now,
which is worryingly and gloriously unique.
There is just the path we walk in all relationships,
between the 'going wrong' and the 'coming right'.

MASTER OF DISGUISE

When war is declared,
the battle on,
and the conflict bitter,
warm loving feelings toward my opponent are scarce.

But what if love doesn't always have
to be a warm feeling?
What if, in conflict, love might just look like a bit of
respect for the one I'm trying to destroy?
Respect which says:
'humanize – don't demonize'.

Love. It looks different in different situations.
Master of disguise.

THE PROMISED LAND

In the Bible,
God promised the children of Israel
good things in the promised land.
Fine wine.
Gorgeous grain.
Sensuous oil.

I hope good things come to you today.
A little bit of promised land is nice.
And you deserve it . . .

GOLDFISH 0 – LOVE 1

With a memory of only three seconds,
a goldfish doesn't have much of an agenda
when you meet.

No festering resentments, for instance.
There just hasn't been time.

But a goldfish has more of an agenda than love.
Love has no agenda.
Carries no baggage.
Love forgets itself completely.
Which is why it is so good to meet.

*Most rows at home start within fifteen minutes
of people getting in, when agendas and baggage
from the day are thrown around with terrible abandon.*

THE ORANGE SURROUND

If you are a painter of very large bridges
across huge rivers,
you will know that by the time you finish,
it's time to start again.
You *never* finish, basically.
And this can be depressing.

So on-site bridge-trained counsellors
recommend the daily celebration
of small good achieved.
The fresh green trap door, for instance,
with bright orange surround,
on the elevated section
of the second of the eight central columns.
I did that!
Excellent. Good. Well done.

All this is also true for those learning love.
Celebrate the small things achieved.

And the fact that *you* don't have to endure an
on-site counsellor . . .

 # FORGIVE ME

Forgive me, but I'm finding it
very hard to accept.
Very hard to accept that I might
not be all you need.
That I might just be *part* of your
picture.
I so wanted to be the *whole*
picture.
I so wanted to be everything
you needed . . .

UNLOADING

It's in families that most of the
worst things are done.
In families, crap is unloaded.
Pile upon pile.
After all,
why need we care?
They're stuck with us.
They're going nowhere.
We can get away with it with them.

Wonderful things, families.
They enable us to be so nice to our friends.

 ROAD DRILL

The old lady was worried by the noise
of the road drills outside.
I wasn't surprised.
They'd been there for two weeks, incessant.
Would have driven me to despair.
Or to violence.
'I don't know how you put up with it,' I said.

'Oh, it's not me I'm worried about,' she replied –
'it's the poor man with the drill.
Fancy doing that for a job.
Imagine having to live with that racket
every day of your life.'

I didn't and I hadn't, to be honest.

*Love. It's putting myself in other people's shoes.
Even when they have a drill in their hands.*

 **STONE**

Stones don't flow.
Whereas water does.

'Let virtue flow through you!' declares the preacher.
The trouble is, they're preaching to stones.
Not water.

Our present psychological position.
Our interior.
It's stony. It's rocky.
And stones and rocks don't flow anywhere.
Before anything good can flow through us,
stone must become water,
the rocks, fluid.

Imagine if the preacher could help us with *that*!
Useful for the first time in their little life.
For then virtue might just become possible.
Wow!

So are you going to tell them?
Or shall I?

A LOAD OF BALZAC

Balzac. Eccentric genius.
Designed and built a house,
but forgot to leave room for a staircase.
Ooops!
Had to be added on afterwards.

The things we forget.
So here's a reminder list for today.
Don't forget to eat. Or you'll faint.
Don't forget to breathe. Or you'll die.
And don't forget to love,
with simple acts of kindness,
or the only staircase to heaven most
people have will be denied them.
Ooops!

 **I BELIEVE**

Some people think that love is
a single boat of relationship.

Some people think that
love is a single river of experience.

Some people think that
love is just one exploration.

I believe love is many boats.
Many rivers.
Many explorations.

And an invitation to all.

A TOTAL ECLIPSE

The relationship.
It was very committed.
Very serious.
Very solid.
Very durable.
Very lasting.
Very permanent.
And very lots of other words
in Roget's thesaurus, which
mean similar things.

Of course it imploded after
27 years, and they split up.

It wasn't their fault, mind.
No.
For it later became apparent
that their relationship coincided
with an almost total eclipse of the fun.

*When laughter leaves,
it takes the future with it.*

LOVE'S SPECIAL DAY

It's Valentine's Day,
and we've got all the lurve-gear:

We've got the Drink-to-me-only
personalized champagne flutes;
the Girl's-best-friend diamanté hair grips;
the soft-on-him silk heart-pattern boxer shorts;
the kiss-kiss vermilion luxury moisturizing lipstick.

And oh yes – the, er, passion fruit
flavoured condom. Pack of three.
How thoughtful.

Yep. It's Valentine's Day,
and we've got all the lurve-gear!

So the starving, the ugly, and the lonely –
they'll have to wait until tomorrow.

Or whenever.

THE MASK AND THE MIRROR

The mask is the keeper of secrets.
The mirror reveals what's there.
the mask can pretend till
the cows come home.
The mirror remains
love's great dare.

It may be in the darkest times,
it may be in the best,
but love will bid us lose the mask,
and face the mirror's test.

Do you like what you see?

THE CAN OF WORMS

When we come across a can of worms
in our life, the first thing to do
is to thank God.
Indeed.

Because just imagine how nasty
it all might have got,
if it *hadn't* been discovered and opened.
The festering! The smell!

It really doesn't bear thinking about.

AN ABSOLUTE WASTE OF TIME

So what's an absolute waste of time?
That's right.
Telling a bald man hair-raising stories.
But if having done that, you have more
time to waste, why not spend the rest of the day
justifying the way you behave,
and judging others accordingly?
Make yourself right. And them wrong.
Because that's an absolute waste of time as well,
solving nothing and creating nothing.
(Apart from hell, of course,
and we don't need more of that.
There's been an over-order in that department already.)

Sometimes love is *not* doing things. See above.

 SAFETY LAST

Safety first.
How wise.
Especially when you are teaching
a child to ride a bike.
Or cross a road.

Or when you're out on the road yourself.
Or mountain climbing. Abseiling. Pot-holing.
Safety first.
Absolutely.
How wise.

But safety first as a *life principle*?
No.
Not wise.
You will narrow.
You will smother.
You will deaden.
You will kill.

*The regret of old age is much more likely
to be concerned with what we didn't do,
than with what we did.*

THE FLOWER SELLER

It's lovely being a flower seller.
To see lovers saying it with flowers.
Ooh look! Here comes Johnny Office-worker!

A single red rose to be sent to his wife.
What a sweetie!
How touching.
He's remembered.
She'll like that.

And of course she'll never know that
he also remembered 12 red roses
for his secretary.
In fact, he personally chose those.
He'll pay cash.
Thought he might.

As I say, it's lovely being a flower seller.
To see lovers saying it with flowers.
Saying everything.

THE LONG GOODBYE

When I can't quite say goodbye.
When I can't quite leave.
When I try and draw the line,
but then my hand reaches out again.

One more touch.
One more word.
One more hug.
One more stretching out of this moment.

You must go.
I must go.
But somehow I can't.

Such fear of the separation.
Such pain of past lost love.
Way back.
Way back when?

BELOW THE WATERLINE

There's more of the iceberg below
the waterline than above it.
The tree's roots burrow further than its
branches climb skywards.
The oceans are deeper than the
mountains are high.

And more hidden, buried, and deeper
than all three are the memories,
from which your present struggle
to love must grow.

Be gentle on yourself.
There's much within,
you know very little about.

 I SURRENDER

New notes are rarely struck by one-man bands.
Columbus set out for wherever because
exploration and discovery was the climate,
the buzz, the wine-bar whisper.
The energy for adventure was there in the community.
And he drank the energy in. As well as the wine.

The surrender of self to those around,
the dismantlement of the one-man band,
the end of an attitude of separation,
is an important part of the adventure of love.
We may not discover America.
But that's no bad thing.

Once was quite enough.

A BEDTIME PRAYER

The mother holds the little figure
and together they pray:

'Cuddle me, hold me, cuddle me tight.
Cuddle me close before you turn out the light.
Hold me a moment, hold me to show
your love will stay with me,
long after you go.
Cuddle me, hold me, cuddle me tight.
Cuddle me close as we both face the night.'

Then she tiptoes out, leaving
the Regius Professor of Divinity at Oxford University
to sleep.

*Nice that he grew up, knowing the difference
between childish – and child-like.*

 THE QUESTION

There's a question at the back of my kind.
I don't want to face it. But here it is:

Which frightens me more:
the terror of not being loved?
Or the terror of loving?

The terror of the huge loneliness
of being special to no one?
Or the terror of committing myself wholeheartedly
to another with no guarantee of return?

Which, in short, is easier?
The isolation of the unloved?
Or the faith required to offer love? . . .

# A GOBSTOPPER?

Here's a gobstopper if you'll
be my best friend,
said the unpopular little boy
as I ran past his classroom.

But I had friends already.
So inwardly, I laughed. And ran on.
I had games to play. I was in demand.

But somehow, the game finished.
And these days, many years on, it's me on the corner,
offering the gobstopper –
a meal out?
a trip to the cinema? –
and wondering if I'll ever make the connection.

 **EROTICA**

I was there to watch the football.
Come on you reds!
That sort of thing.
But the woman next to me
was more vocal about
our striker's nice tight bum, and magnificent thighs.

Like me watching the women's 200 metres.
I'm not really there for a commonwealth record.

But erotic is bigger than bum.
It's also about what the other represents.
The way she receives, creates, protects,
endures, nurtures, and stays with reality.
The way he penetrates, guides, disciplines, imagines.

Deep psychic symbols.
And the longing to score.

Meanwhile back at the football . . .

I DO

In the registry office,
everyone was dressed in Dracula outfits.
Expensive. But fun.
And they wanted it to be fun.

The young couple said I do.
The girl was saying I do want a baby.
The boy was saying I do want a laugh.
The bridesmaid giggled nervously.
She hoped she might be next with the boy.
The slightly drunk uncle swore at the video,
which had just jammed.
Knew his way around the place.
He'd been married here at least three times.
And in the meantime, Celine Dion sings –
or is it Whitney Houston? Or Mariah Carey?
Still, it's a love song.
That's the main thing.

Because obviously today is all about love . . .

 SPECIAL

First there was Michael.
Then there was Chris.
Followed shortly by Dino and then Frank.
Then came Kevin.
Nice boy.
And then David.
Then Steve.
And then, of course, you!

Me? Ahhh!

Then John, Peter, Mel – who was brilliant –
Leslie, Eric, Charlie, Tony, Eddie, Caspar, Jim . . .

* * *

Some people have a great gift in making you feel special.
And some people *don't*.

 CLUBBIN' IT

In the card game of life,
there are some who think
that Clubs are trumps:
all that force and power.
And some think that Diamonds are trumps:
all that lovely wealth.
Whilst others back Spades:
dogged hard work.
That should do the trick.

I think Jesus felt that
Hearts were trumps.
Which is probably why
they ripped his heart to pieces.

*Because previous to that assault,
he'd had a pretty good hand.
Including the ace . . .*

NO, *REALLY!* . . .

The psychopath.
The murderer.
The child molester.
The tyrant.
The torturer.
The bully.
The manipulator.
The liar.
The racist.
The stockbroker.

They're all good people.
Somewhere.

Oh. And so are you.
Yes, you.
No, *really*!
You are.
Well, don't look so surprised!

 **IF I WAS YOU**

If I was you,
I wouldn't do that.
I mean, if I was in your shoes,
there's no way I'd do what you're doing.

But you're not me.

No, but if I was.
Standing where you stand.
Looking as you look,
feeling as you feel.

But you can't stand where I stand, look as I look,
Or feel as I feel.

Oh come on –
you can't hide behind all that stuff and nonsense for ever.
No. If I was you –

If you were me,
you'd decide to become more like you.
Yes?
Why is difference so hard for you?

 # WHAT TO PRAY

I blame idolatry.
It's idolatry which gets us into the mess.

Idolatry is the giving of *absolute* value
to something of *relative* worth.
And so it is with young love.
In its energy and confidence, it is blind.
It invents. Passionately, hopelessly, dangerously.
And then it falls, inebriated, for its own invention.
Oh dear.

For the passing seasons take their savage toll.
The drunk sobers up, and in the cold light of day,
the absolute has become a little relative.
The trouble is, by then –
some couples are left holding a baby.
Oh dear.

Pray you never see through the invention.
Or pray for strength when you do.

SPADEWORK

Beware when you hear spades
being brought out of the cupboard.
Beware when you see the land being
surveyed with smug eyes by the foreman.
Beware when the digging starts,
and the pits appear,
and the raised earth platform is built.

In short, beware the building of
moral high ground from which to speak.

Between pit and pulpit,
between high ground and low,
there is no conversation,
no communication,
no communion,
no good.

A TOUCH SIMPLE

You know the sort of things.
Holy relics.
The actual nails used
to crucify Christ. Yes?
Or wood from Noah's ark.
The original crown of thorns.
A sandal worn by St Peter.
A chunk of wood from the cross.
Of course.

Yet as the bent lady in black touched, she whispered love
to the God who before had seemed so far away.
As she touched, she felt the fall of the separating curtain,
and the distant divine, now close.

Stupid old bat.
Being taken in like that.
One sad relic touching another.
She must be a touch simple.

Maybe. Though love needs touch.
She may just be a touch in love.

SEX AND THE SOUTH DOWNS

I love the South Downs,
but I wouldn't want to have sex with them.

I love Manchester United,
but I wouldn't want to go for long walks over them.

I love fish and chips,
but I wouldn't queue to see them play Arsenal.

I love my children,
but I don't cover them in vinegar.

I love God,
but I don't pray for his future happiness.

I love my partner,
but I don't place my life in her hands.

And as I say, I love the South Downs,
but I don't want to have sex with them.

Love. There's a lot of it out there.
And each time, it looks a little different.

IT'S ALL IN THE PREPARATION

So I put down the magazine.
And I turn off the radio.
And the telly next door.
And just for once I don't pour myself a drink.
Or light a cigarette.

But just sit. Alone.
And I feel restless.
This is clearly a complete waste of time.
A thousand thoughts spring to mind.
Two thousand anxieties.
And half a dozen half-baked plans.

So I try and listen to my breathing.
Which is apparently what keeps me alive.
And gradually become aware of the little
universe who is me.
And which I control. Today.

It's a discipline, yes.
But if I can't be alone with myself,
I'm really not fit to be with anyone else.

# KITCHEN SINK

At the height of the row in the kitchen,
she had no fear for herself,
but she did fear for the children.

At the height of the row in the kitchen,
the children strangely feared nothing –
for they saw the strength in her.

And amidst the sharp knives,
the smashed glass,
the dead dreams,
love, weak and battered,
seeped and swirled strong between them.

Love stronger than kitchen danger.

PUTTING ON THE KETTLE

Forgiveness,
if it comes at all,
is rarely a moment.
But rather, a process.

Like the coming of the dawn,
it's often very hard to say exactly *when*
it happens.
Hard to say a precise *now*.

However, while we're awaiting the dawn,
there's much good we can do.
We can still *act* as children of the light.
Even if it's dark.
We could put the kettle on. Do the washing up.

And likewise,
while we're awaiting the strength to forgive,
there's still much to be done.
And indeed, *not* done.
Like kneecapping people, for instance . . .

THE EXCEPTION

They can take everything from us.
They can smash down our doors,
break our windows, and take
what they want.
They can use our bodies,
cut, break or rape.
They can possess our minds
with a few well-chosen drugs.
They can have the lot,
by force, by blackmail, by pressure applied.

Except our love of course.
No one can take that.
Not even God.
Love, we have to *give*.

 **SOLO?**

You know I'll be there for you.
You know that whatever happens,
I'll drop everything. You just need to say.
I'll come running.
And I'll be strong.
Strong and steady,
amidst your falling apart;
the calm amidst the crisis.
I'll face your demons, and insist
the angels walk with you.

I've said it all a thousand times.
I'll be there. Believe.

But that isn't what I really want to say.
This is what I fear to ask.
'Will *you* be there for *me*?'

Or is this love flying solo?

 # HARD LINES

Here's to you – without me:

Shine like a diamond, even though
others will then count you as one of their jewels.
Fly like an eagle, even though it means
I must uncup the hands which have held you.
Be a friend to the world, even though it
feels like a knife stab to *our* friendship.
Need others, as I need others.
Grow as a person beyond the small
horizons I offer you.

I cry as I write.
Each line is a wrench.
I can't let go.
But you must leave.
I love you.

GREAT INVENTIONS

With each loving word uttered at the funeral, the church
became increasingly airless, drained of
the oxygen of reality . . .

'. . . he was marvellous. A diamond. Never a cross word.
Nicest man you could hope to meet.
Kept himself to himself, of course.
But would do anything for anybody.
Wouldn't want us to cry.
He was a saint, that man.'

But afterwards, in the vestry:
'I've cleared his room, vicar.
Best done quick, I reckon.
Oxfam take old clothes, don't they?
To be honest, he was a miserable old sod.'

To be honest.
That's where love starts from.
Not with invention.

 A LOVE SONG

It's when I hate you that I find it hard to love.
When I wish you a thousand miles away.
When what you do revolts me,
bores me, leaves me cold.

Once you could hurt me.
More than once you did.
But no more. Not now.
I'm too cold to feel. Too numb.
And two's a crowd.

Tied unfeeling to this terrible winter,
pinned to this frozen ground,
and the years stretch out ahead.
So long.
So long.

It's when I hate you that I find it hard to love.

 # THE SECRET

The old man squeezed the tea bag
against the side of the cup.
She liked it strong.
And not too much milk.
It was 5.30 a.m.
And he'd made her tea, at this time,
for 43 years.

They'd done other things as well.
They'd been to Paris. Probably a mistake.
They'd had oral sex. Another mistake.
They'd brought up two children.
They'd shared various illnesses.
Moved home twice.
Been to Rhyl, Southend and Eastbourne.
Other places too.

But mainly it had been tea.
Or that's how it seemed.
Brewed strong, at 5.30 a.m.
Every morning for 43 years.

Not too much milk.
That was the secret.

 CLOSURE

How do you know when a fire has gone out?
Is it when the flames die?
Or when the embers cease to glow?
Or when the last faltering spark of
orange-red is killed cold by the cooling ash?
At what point is a fire beyond saving?
When exactly do you declare a fire dead?

And when do you declare a love dead?
How many rows, how much violence,
how long the silences, how many the lies? –
how damaged the broken bridges,
before we say,
'This partnership is done'?

When that being destroyed
outweighs that being created –
maybe then love takes its coat from the hook in the hall,
and steps out into the night.

Goodbye.

 # TERRIBLE

So it's a story Jesus told of this young man who
walked out on his dad, demanding the money
he would have received in his will, *now*.
Calculating, insensitive, hurtful.

Having received the money, he disappeared off,
spent it, thinking of no one, feeling for no one,
until he found himself broke and face down
in the gutter. It was then he thought of his dad.
Surprise, surprise.
Surely he couldn't return home? Not after
what he'd done . . .

The gutter, however, was persuasive. He *did* start home.
But before he got there, something terrible happened.
His father, seeing him coming, rushed out
and hugged him before he could say a word.

Falling into the arms of love, with no chance to explain.
Terrible. As in, terribly good.

 # MIXED

Please.
Don't ever try and purify your motives.
Don't even think about it.
Complete waste of time.
Your motives. They're mixed. Always will be.

So don't even try and be pure.
But do keep your wayward motives
in front of you.
Within your gaze.

They generally do less damage there.

 NO CANE DO

Did your dad cane you?

Never – he had a big hardback book on child psychology.

Must have been great.

No. He used to smack me round the head with that instead.

* * *

Tend your heart.
Not your bookshelf.

GENERALLY SPEAKING . . .

It's better not to shout at the children
It's better not to hope others fail
It's better not to deal out the judgement
It's better not to bang in that nail
It's better not to strut like a peacock
It's better not to wall up your mind
It's better to be big and say sorry
It's better not to pull down the blinds

It's better not to tread on your neighbour
It's better not to muffle her cry
It's better not to outdo Mr Busy
It's better if it's you who must die
It's better to step out than to sit there
It's better to encourage than complain
Here's hoping that you lift and don't shackle
Here's hoping you're both sunshine and rain

And I hear this wisdom
come down from above
It's better not to live
than not to love

JUST WONDERING

She loves me, she loves me not.
He loves me, he loves me not.
She loves me, she loves me not.
He loves me, he loves me not.
She loves me, she loves me not.
He loves me, he loves me not.
She loves me, she loves me not.
He loves me, he loves me not.
She loves me, she loves me not.
He loves me, he loves me not.

Honestly.
Hasn't God got better things
to do than play with that bloody dandelion all day?

 HELPLESS

It's terrible when we are helpless.
It's terrible when there's nothing we can do.
But there are few such inspirers of community,
few such inspirers of love, as the helpless.

Once the child had screamed in the street below,
the business meeting couldn't quite
get back on track.
We'd all rushed to the window.
We'd all felt the pain of the helpless cry,
the little wailing hands beating on the door,
shut out, shit scared . . .

We'd resumed our seats.
Resumed our important business.
But it wasn't the same.
We were a community now.

Maybe one day, I'll be the helpless one.
Maybe sooner rather than later.
And maybe love will be created around me.

WHEN THE DREAM ENDS

Shelley, the poet.
He knew the difference, I think.
Between longing and love.
Longing is ache, longing is distance.
The desire of the moth for the star,
the ache of the night for the morrow,
the devotion to something afar,
from the sphere, from the place of our sorrow.

If rejected, longing can quick become hate.
If allowed to fester, sick infatuation.
But if the longing is granted, then what?
If the ache is appeased, the distance travelled,
and we actually get what we want?
Then longing *may* become love.

Love is living the cost of arrival.
The dream is over.
The real-life adventure begins.

 LAME LOVE

Brother Lawrence, born Nicholas Herman
in Lorraine in the seventeenth century, was converted
by a tree at the age of 18 – stripped bare in
winter, then a few months later, all fruit and flowers.
Stunned youthful amazement.
And a light went on inside.

Well, it worked for *him* anyway.
And from that day on, he decided to make
the love of God the end of all his actions.
Even picking up a piece of straw from the ground.
Or going to Burgundy to collect wine for his religious order.
He had no head for business, *and* he was lame,
which made the boat travel hard.
But in the name of love . . .

Tree experience or no tree experience.
God or no God.
In the name of love.
Every action.
The story goes on . . .

LOVE AND FEAR

I think if I could pause,
relax,
let my breathing slow,
and lie down in the holding heart of God –
then I might experience what
Jesus said:
perfect love casts out fear.

Who knows?

A TITANIC DISCOVERY

You'll remember the bit in the film.
He can't hold on for much longer.
He's about to go under.
He's about to drift into freezing watery oblivion.
A few last words with the one he loves . . .

He'd won at poker to get on the cruise.
Won a ticket to his death.
Some might say that was a winning
they could live without.
But he'd also won a ticket
to the discovery of love.

And so he's able to say with his dying breath,
It was worth it.

I hope I can say that before I slip under.
I hope you can.